W9-AOJ-322

YELLOW DOG JOURNAL

YELLOW DOG JOURNAL

Poems by Judith Minty

PARALLAX PRESS
BERKELEY, CALIFORNIA

ACKNOWLEDGMENTS

Sections 1, 2, 5, 7, 8, 9, 22, 23, 24 from Fall Sequence
first appeared in *Poetry 1979*, the Modern Poetry Association.

Several poems from the Spring Sequence first appeared
in *Hawaii Review* and in *Black Warrior Review*.

Yellow Dog Journal was originally published by
Center Publications, Los Angeles, California.
Copyright 1979 by Judith Minty.
Reprinted by Parallax Press, 1991.

Cover Design by Lawrence Watson
Cover Photograph courtesy LTA Publishing Portland, Oregon
Printed in the U.S.A.
ISBN 0-938077-85-6

PARALLAX PRESS
P.O. Box 7355
Berkeley, California 94707

For my father, Karl Jalmer Makinen.
And for my Aunts Martha, Lynn,
Katherine and Bertha, and my Uncle Harold.

With Appreciation to Jack Driscoll, Cynthia Nibbelink
and Diane Wakoski for reading this poem in its early stages.
And to the Yaddo Corporation, where I was able to complete it.

Contents

FOREWORD

Judith Minty taught me how to walk in the woods. Now, mind you, not everyone can teach. Even those who have all the information and the experience cannot necessarily teach. To teach one has to hold the understanding so deeply within her that it has become an intrinsic part of her—it *is* her, so to speak. When Judith Minty walks in the woods she meets the woods on its own terms. Consequently, the woods are in her and she is in them; she allows herself to become part of the mud, the light, the wind, and the bear.

Judith taught me how to see. She taught me how to be so silent that I disappeared before the song of the bird. She taught me that the creatures I observed are themselves the sacred inhabitants of a sacred world which requires awareness and an open heart to enter. And she taught me this rigorous meditation practice—and the names of trees and animals, the signatures of their prints and scat—without a word of rhetoric, because she taught me as a poet teaches.

Such are these poems. They teach us how to enter the woods. They teach us that the woods are a sacred world from which we have exiled ourselves and into which we may sometimes return. They describe the path—and its ordeals—through which we may enter the deep, dark woods, for these poems also detail a descent and a return. We descend, as Judith did, stripped by the four elements of earth, fire, wind, and water in order to confront the bear, that fearsome dream animal, "black coat bristling, eyes burning" who calls and frightens us at the edge of the clearing, that force of nature which we must nakedly pursue and escape. And then she takes us back, after the fall of descent during the rising of spring "as darkness settles/[and] only trillium blossoms/and the bark of birch trees/hold the light."

Oh, in these times, it is indeed a privilege to walk in the woods. Let this poet lead you as she leads me and take to heart these bare and eloquent poems which transmit the teachings of the natural world in its seasons, its elements, and its four directions.

—Deena Metzger
Topanga, California
November 1991

Go, my daughter, to discover
Why the grey-brown dog is barking,
And the long-eared dog is baying.
　　　　　—Runo XVIII
　　　　　　Kalevala

YELLOW DOG JOURNAL

FALL

Welcome, Bear, be thy coming,
Honey-pawed, who now approachest
To our dwelling, freshly-scoured,
To our household, now so charming.
    This I wished for all my lifetime,
All my youth I waited for it.
                —Runo XLVI
                Kalevala

1

400 miles into north land, driving hard
like a runaway, each town peeling away the woman skin,
turning me pale and soft, as if I
had never married, had not
been planted twenty years in the suburbs.

I come here as my father's child, back
down his rutted road, through a cave of sagging timber
to the clearing. Nothing changed.
His land, his shack leaning over the riverbank,
the Yellow Dog barking home to Superior.

2

This cabin has not been lived in
since August. October now, and rain
crawls over trees, roof. It muddies the trail.

Bone cold, I light the stove. Damp
shrivels into seams of the walls
and all the flies of summer burst alive again.

They beat their wings against the windows.
They whine and bleat in a confusion of seasons,
then cling to shadows on the ceiling.

I swing at them with a newspaper, wonder
how long I'll last here.
Maple leaves dry yellow on my boots.

3

My father's slippers, found
in a trunk, now mine to wear.
Too large, creases in the leather
barely touch the flesh.
I slide my toes to the end, along the old ridges.

His feet clump over linoleum floor
table to dishpan, woodbox to stove.
Only the scrap of rug by the door
muffles his presence.

4

Night comes early in October.
I prop my feet up,
lean into the old rocker.
Rain flows over the roof.
Flames from the wood stove
spin off walls, ceiling,
circle the amber in my glass,
this shack a hive humming.

5

Last night I drank too much and, almost
asleep, thought of old lovers.
Decided I would hike three miles
to a phone in the morning, call a friend. Ask him
to come north, drive nine hours into autumn.

Today the sky is clear, the trees on fire.
I tie a scarf around my head and walk
to the river for water.

6

All day, I stay close to the cabin.
My ax rings the morning. And half the afternoon
I gather kindling, spread the sticks
to dry. I am menstruating and have heard
that bear are attracted to women when they bleed.

I haven't spoken in three days, have seen nothing
bigger than chipmunks and squirrels
at the woodpile. It is only beyond the perimeter
that black shapes hide, breath steaming,
low growls circling their throats.
When the branch falls, I swirl to the sound, ax raised.

7

Sitting on the porch.
Can't tell if I was dozing or reading,
the eye had wandered from words,
turned inward,
so that I only saw it
after the chipmunk's scream.

The hawk spread its wings,
so close I might have touched his feathers,
and lifted the chipmunk up
out of the clearing
and made no sound.

8

At first, I think they are dogs trailing bear.
I run to the door, that old dream:
copper fur trundling low to my ground,
circling, yelping. The bear
crashing through brush into my clearing,
black coat bristling, eyes burning.

But the clearing is empty. I had forgotten
about geese flying south. Now they bark
across the sky, great packs, sometimes sixty in formation,
silver wingtips over the Yellow Dog,
flowing in and out like white water.
I stand on the porch, dinner fork still in my hand.

9

The stories that stay with you.
Like Sally's, about the bear
that looked in at her while she was looking out.

This cabin has no curtains.
What's the point,
there are no people here.
But tonight fur rises on my neck
when the bear bawls for Mother and all I see is
an aging woman at my window.

10

He left this land in the thirties,
left the aunts growing old in Ishpeming,
three sisters without men now
who stir inside the walls of their past.
They want to end where they began
in the house of their childhood.

He was the oldest brother,
the engineer downstate in Detroit.
Had he stayed, he would have been
a logger, or maybe burst his lungs in the mine.
Summers, he'd cast out for trout,
with no time left for visiting women.

It was he told me the Yellow Dog,
made my sleep spin into the woods, to the falls
above the clearing, the ore shining gold in the sun.
Late nights, he'd whisper its bends,
my face close to his Finnish gutteral,
cheeks flushed from his beard's rough stubble.

11

Beavers gone, but their lodge remains,
broken in the pond. I walk
the edge, sink through twigs and mud,
then circle back to path again. The water
has no motion, like a dream suspended.

Across from me, two birch trees
spring alive in the reflection. They grow out
of clarity. I fall away from the depth of it
and wish someone there to catch me,
to hold me from the roots.

Although I never hear the plane, I catch
its jet stream, born below the birch branches.
It lifts clearly off the surface.
All the way back to the cabin, I
tell myself, "This happened in water."

12

Thinking how good it is
to come up the path from the river,
chimney smoke sifting above the trees,
to open the cabin door and find myself
still there, stirring logs in the stove.

13

Crazy. Crazy woman.
    I've stopped combing my hair.
    Now I whisper in the cabin
    and cross myself at dusk.
Crazy. Crazy woman.
    Tonight, on the porch,
    I unbutton my shirt, let my breasts
    swim in the full moon's light.

14

The raven shrieks.
His shadow cuts the river, west to east,
when I dip my bucket for water.

15

Now a dog has followed me home.
I hiked three miles north
to the nearest neighbor
to ask if they'd give me wood.
No one home but the beagle puppy.

Tomorrow I'll have to walk
that damned dog back again.
Meanwhile he keeps me warm,
snoring inside my sleeping bag.

16

Gathering wood today:
rotten logs, twigs, fallen branches.
One knapsack holds six hours of heat,
I mutter, hike
the long trail back
sweating in the afternoon sun.

17

I miss that beagle. He was spooky
alright, wouldn't stray
more than fifty yards, and scared of the dark.
But he came at a whistle
and curled tight just above my knees
in the middle of the night.

18

This is the dawn I want
to fly out of here. I have already
emptied the drawer, folded underwear into my pack.
I stand in the chill,
the half-light, wondering what
foolishness made me leave the familiar.

"Your house is on fire, your children will burn."

All night, I slept sitting up.
Through my open window, I saw
trees walking. Black prowlers of the woods
whispered warning, knocked in code on the shingles.
Bats whirred a wind above my head and tiny feet
gained entry, scratched and squealed along the floor.

"Wait. It is not finished yet."

The sun slouches over the yellowing birch grove.
I bend at the woodbox, my breath
beating in puffs. Soon I will sweep the floor,
the mouse droppings left in the dark.

19

When a forest burns, animals
gather by water. Now the sun
catches leaves in a blossom of fire.
In this setting, I doze
and when the crackling comes, I believe
in a growling and screeching that snag my breath.

At the river, I kneel and cup my hands
to drink. Behind me, the bear
rattles his throat,
rears up, charges. His claws
rake my back and I fall into heat.

Grit of sand and water, flames
snapping, his breath
this weight to bear.
I know the bleeding
only comes from inside, but far away
my daughter cries out with her own dream of it.

20

Someone has been fishing my hole.
I find footprints at the river.
Two of them.
A father and son, perhaps?
A husband and wife? Lovers?
When they come together up the path,
I'll be waiting on the porch.

Christ!
Next I'll be stringing barbed wire.

21

When the sun falls,
oaks pull in their branches
and shadows
creep closer to the cabin.
I am never alone in these woods.

22

All day. Now night
and the sky still clear. I can see
parts of a constellation. Perhaps
it is Orion raising his sword
as leaves open tiny doorways for me.

If I were not so afraid
in the dark, tonight
I would walk to the beaver pond.
Never looking over my shoulder, just poking
down the trail, blind woman
with her stick in a world without shadows.
I would come to it on this night.

And the stars: The stars
would gleam first above me,
then reflect in the still water.
I would look down at the bear
and the dog star in Canis
and see that the pond runs deep
as the night sky. And know this.
Tonight. If I had no fear of it.

23

In the dream the bear is inside
the house of my childhood.
My mother, a woman poet, my daughter
all push against a bulging door.
They are trying to keep the bear in the basement,
but I can see his huge, scruffy head, his rubber nose,
his black, matted coat through the opening.

In the dream the bear is chasing me
through all the rooms of my house.
The two of us bounce in great, airy jumps
from bed to bed. He is breaking all the furniture.
When I run to the outer door and yank it open, his woods
sink into a hole. I hesitate,
then slam the door, wait for his paws to take me.

Awake, sweat gathers in my palms,
the moon opens on my ceiling, and my heart
beats as if I had been climbing the ravine.
The *mh, mh, mh, mh* from the bear's throat
still echoes in the cabin. It is only
draft from the stove as embers cool.
When I was a child, I never dreamed
I'd have to hold this beast inside.

24

Once, in anger, my mother said
no man would marry me if I kept
my mean disposition.
Now my own daughters scowl and turn
their eyes to men, and my husband
has a heart big enough to hold a month of tantrums.

Still, I come here without them
and turn into this crone, this old woman
who hobbles on her stick along the riverbank,
who mutters deep in her throat
and smells of bear,
who combs her fingers through her hair
and cackles when leaves float down in front of her.

It is almost time. There is no one
who remembers the child, except perhaps
the animals who breathe softly around her.

Harsh throat of the falls,
two bends away, half a mile
from my cabin door.

Groping down the ravine
on a stairway of tree roots,
the roar rising, I sink
into pines, the pitch smell lifting,
the stream rushing down.

Woman opens to man.
Mouth, arms, thighs soft as petals.
She waits for him to enter
the flower of her.

I climb out on rock,
center of the rapids,
white water boiling, wind
drowning, a thunder
everywhere. Everything
stops breathing.

Long after he leaves, she holds
the wet seed of him, his child
swimming in her darkness.

Boulder below, big as a bear,
crooked pine on the opposite bank,
maple leaf held in the pool.
No shadow, but the fall
of water. All motion caught
blazing in the sun.

When my daughter was born
I wept for three days,
I did not want her
to leave the secret place.

26

Only light in this cabin is inside
the stove, pine knots
aged how many months, years.
Part of place, like the trout
trapped by falls who fatten and giggle
until they flop off the line, until
the tiny heave of the fisherman's heart dies.

I have captured this wood.
Tonight, its spirit swims in flame.
Dorsal fin, snagged
in the bright river, shivers, glows
until eye dissolves before my eyes.
Can fire bring us alive then?

I rise out of apathy, out of my chair
to the stove, burning
for wet scales, the quiver of gills.
Inside, I know I am
already leaving these woods,
swimming away from shadows
down the highway, another kind of homing.

27

These trees are past their prime.
Over sixty feet tall, lower branches
stripped of needles, roots
heaved up, bent like arthritic hands.

I fill the front of my shirt
with pine cones. Later, when I rock
on the porch, nodding my head,
I will smell the floor of the woods.

28

I tried to bury it,
but it's surfaced now.
When the dog slept with me
he was my father.

29

I am standing in the dump, in back
of the outhouse, with all
the tired things that refuse to decompose.
Plastic jugs, booze bottles, old cans,
the rusted carcass of a stove.

I am digging a grave, three feet by one.
It could hold a child or an animal.
My shovel is long-handled, its blade
nicked and caked with dirt.
It clanks against rocks and my breath
catches when I heave them out.
This is timberland, never meant to be farmed.

In the morning, before I leave these woods,
I will fill this hole and cover it over.
But tonight, sweating from my own effort, my own
animal odor rising, I step away from the hole.
Never looking over my shoulder,
I roll back on these haunches
and let the long, shrill howl rise.
It runs out like a song from my throat.

SPRING

Hail, O Moon, who beamest yonder....
   Go ye on your path with blessings,
Go ye on your charming journey,
Let your crescent now be beauteous,
Rest ye joyful in the evening.
         —Runo XLIX
         Kalevala

1

No clouds for a week. May,
yet this day belongs to summer.
I have bolted my house
to race north again to woods
that lace the light with new leaves.

Still here. Still here.
Snow holds near the bank,
the Yellow Dog runs full at the bend.
I sing over bumps and puddles,
homing back to the old clearing.

2

Washout. Road sliced in two
where the swale met a frozen drain,
still water risen from lowland.

Oh glory to feet!
I haul books, food and shirts
the last half mile on my back.

3

Dusk, the moon waxing
to clarity, trillium and violets
exploding everywhere.

Across the river
a million frogs
fill their throats with song.

4

I hear it in the river first
and step outside. This rain
has not climbed my hill yet.
Then, tiny pricks
on the roof. It begins.
Water over water: a perfect time
for love, all the creatures
hiding under leaves.
Alone on the porch, I
whisper familiar names to the wind.

5

Mice in the woodbox. The fire
still warm, they must think
I am like Gulliver, either dead
or asleep.
They poke their little heads out,
they rattle over newspapers
to eye this intruder
who writes in their giant bed.
Later, in the dark, they will
tie me here
with fine threads from their nests.

6

Something in the attic.
All night, a ghost
hunts mice above me. I hear
them scurry, then squeal.

It does no good to rise
out of sleep into this cold room.
The hunting comes only
when I sink into dream again.

ז

So cold this morning, my breath
puffs in front of me and my fingers
ache when I hold the pen.
But at least there will be
no rain. Today sun
lights the table top, runs down
to a patch of yellow on my sleeping bag,
skims the floor in dusty streaks.

8

Shooting in the distance:
five shots, then five more.
Breath catches, eyes
jump from the page.

This is Spring, not hunting
season, a time for wildflowers
and mating. I'm sure it is
only boys at target practice.

Still, the doe suspends
her hoof. I will not walk
that hill to the east today.

9

All winter, my poems
were thin and icy, my head
filled with other people's words.
Those dark months, I lived
in the corners of failure.
Now, here by the river,
the hermit thrush opens his throat,
lines flow over the page, the afternoon sun
warms my shoulders, my back
in its slow circle.

10

Oh my friend, I wish you
here with me. This evening
I walked upstream where I have never been,
planning to find the source of Bushey Creek.
But the woods were thick and I could see
many bends above me still.
It was not that I was afraid
of losing my way or that night
would come before I found the spring.
It was that there would be no one
to share the mystery, how water
can bubble up out of earth,
then flow into this delicate stream.
So instead, I sat among moss and lichen,
studied the hill on the opposite bank,
then turned back and headed downstream
toward the thunder of the falls.

11

Violets in a green glass
salt shaker. My face and hands
clean from the river.

I have set a formal table in these woods:
flowers, silverware and wine,
canned beans steaming on my plate.

12

Beaver lodge begun
below where I dip for water.
Twigs and leaves bending out from the bank,
the river so clear I can see down
to where the log holds below the surface.

I track him up to the woods,
the drag mark of his flat tail.

13

Though nearly midnight,
the sky is dawn's, shadows
of trees balanced against gray.
When I step onto the chill porch
to look for her, the moon
is there. Nearly full
she forms a cross through the screen: north, south,
east and west, reaching out
to mark us all in lunacy,
to set us mixing days and nights.

14

Those mice were too bold.
They ran right up to my chair,
across the sink. They peered at me
from around paint cans on the shelf.
Last night I set the traps,
then dreamed I skinned a fox
for the Cherokee woman downstate.
Today I unlock two frozen bodies, look away
from their surprised eyes, try to recall
that woman half-crazed by moonbeams.

15

Monday, lundi, day
of the full moon, the whole world
working at jobs in villages, cities, on farms.
I have saved the poems of Ryokan for this occasion.
Now, as he speaks to me from his hermitage,
I come to it again: we are all related.

16

This good French bread
from the Negaunee bakery
has lasted almost a week.
I tear off a piece, then lather it
with butter. I remember
she apologized it wasn't a long loaf.
No doubt, hearing my downstate accent,
she thought I meant to cut it with a knife.
How could she know my tongue
ached to thank her in the northland gutteral,
that I would kiss the bread before I ate it.

17

After dinner, near the beaver lodge,
I watch an osprey follow the flow
downstream, glide, then lift its wings.
It floats the path of clouds.
Upstream, around the next bend, bats
hang in the saplings waiting for twilight.

18

This water flows, then catches
in little eddies, almost
trying to run upstream again.
Then it hurries on, tugs
at the bush next to me,
nods the twig at the bend.
It plays the same at the falls,
only louder, with a certain fury.
Here, by my father's sandy beach,
the river is surely a contented woman.

19

Twenty years ago, with his big Finnish hands,
my father planted these Yellow Dog pines.
Now the tallest is twice his height, and I
am nearly his age when he put them in the ground.
They fan out around the clearing,
green in all seasons, their scent
light in the breeze from the river,
only a few stunted from the hard winters.

20

Where are the jays this spring?
Now it is the city robin
who is first to call in the morning,
last to sleep at night.

21

Sometimes I think it is
the waterfall, but I know
it is the wind I hear
long before it arrives
at my clearing. West,
the beech trees are calm
as Ojibwa women in their blankets,
then after the sound of it
they begin to sway in quiet
pleasure. At last it is here,
the smell of rain on the way,
the burning left for another season.

22

Again, frogs courting.
First one starts, a violinist
trying his bow across the string,
then two or three more tune up.
Then a symphony, along the riverbank,
out of ponds. And the birds,
hidden in a thousand trees.

23

As darkness settles,
only trillium blossoms
and the bark of birch trees
hold the light.

24

After ten. Waiting,
waiting on the porch.
First sight, a faint sheen
on the opposite bank. White,
then yellow creeping up.
Then gold.
The wind swirls
now from all directions
as the moon lifts
over the pines, the night
sounds chanting it on.

25

Oh moon, full,
oh perfect ball of reflected light,
these crossed haloes
North, South, East, West
your brilliance, light
this page I write on, move
me to know this loneliness
of celebration. Who,
there in the other world, is chanting,
praising you? Who hears them,
those she-wolves, howling
and baying as you rise,
as I open my mouth now,
this shadow singing behind me.

26

Reading the life of Crazy Horse,
then Ryokan's poems. Their
solitude seems natural to me
as I sweep the cabin floor
for the last time this spring.

27

Since I have been here, I have killed
two mice in traps and one bat
I beat to death in the outhouse.
Last night my dreams were colorless.
I think I missed the whir of wings,
the sound of tiny nails on the floor,
fur skimming close to my face. Something
gnaws inside my head. It asks forgiveness.

28

Three ravens screech
and squawk their way
downriver. I remember
when their cry terrified me,
how once they met me
on the road, would barely let me pass,
fluttering their wings,
strutting back and forth.
Now I need no light at night
and walk the trail without a stick,
my feathers nearly formed.

29

When I last dreamed the bear, he rose
from the earth, the trees
parted in his path, twigs snapping, cracking
from his weight, his flesh
swaying as he lumbered up the hill.

When I last dreamed the bear, he climbed
the stairs to my porch, the rough pads
of his feet brushed in whispers
on the wood: my eyes
sliding back into my head when I turned to face him.

When I last dreamed the bear, he laid
his black head on my thigh,
the bear-smell rising rank around us,
his coat bristling my skin,
the great weight of him leaning, leaning into me.

And though we never spoke,
I knew then that he loved me, and so began
to stroke his rough back, to pull him even closer.

30

Here, by this pine or that rock,
near these falls, they cupped their palms with water
like Ripley's father, fisherman turned doctor,
who crooned the words to her.
They dipped their daughters in the stream so that we rose
enchanted, eyes starry in the forest.

No longer theirs, though always theirs
since we fell wet from the mother,
now bound to their place, we come
back and back to follow the current. Each time we stand
breathless on the edge, in this blend
of light and shadow, this river pulsing.